John G Orger

Critical Notes on Shakespeare's Histories and Tragedies

John G Orger

Critical Notes on Shakespeare's Histories and Tragedies

ISBN/EAN: 9783337062958

Printed in Europe, USA, Canada, Australia, Japan

Cover: Foto ©Thomas Meinert / pixelio.de

More available books at **www.hansebooks.com**

CRITICAL NOTES

ON

SHAKSPERE'S HISTORIES AND TRAGEDIES.

BY

JOHN G. ORGER, M.A.,

English Chaplain at Dinan, France; late Rector of Cranford, Northants.

LONDON:
HARRISON AND SONS, 59, PALL MALL, S.W.
Booksellers to the Queen and H.R.H. the Prince of Wales.

1890.

PREFACE.

SOME few of these notes defend the text against change. Some few others suggest change where none has been proposed. The rest are devoted to passages where change is clearly needed, and the conjectures hitherto offered have failed to be satisfactory.

Where emendations have been proposed by others which commend themselves to my own judgment, though they have not secured the suffrages of editors, I have not felt called upon to support their adoption, as I had to suppose their authors did their best to recommend them. These, therefore, I leave aside; together with those passages in which, though no satisfactory explanation or alteration has been discovered, I am conscious I have none to offer.

This will explain the method of selection in the following notes, which I refer to the censure of the Shakspere Student in the hope that some at least of the conjectures offered will merit his consideration.

In the notes on the Comedies published last year, page 23, for the line in *Measure for Measure*, Act iii, 1, 17—

"Yes, he would *give't* thee ; *from* this rank offence,"

I proposed "Yes, he would *quit* thee *of* this rank offence," altering "from" to "of," because, as I said, I could not find "quit from" in use. I avail myself of the preface to this volume to observe that this is needless, as I find what is virtually the same expression in *Richard III*, Act iii, 7, 233—

> Your mere enforcement shall *acquittance* me
> *From* all the impure blots and stains thereof,

which will allow of our reading—

"Yes, he would *quit* thee *from* this rank offence."

I take this opportunity, also, of pointing out an emendation of a passage in the Sonnets, which, though very obvious, has hitherto escaped observation. In *Sonnet* lxv, where the author deplores the effect of Time on Beauty, and illustrates it by its power over "rocks" and "gates of steel," he concludes—

> O Fearful Meditation! Where, alack,
> Shall Time's best jewel from Time's *chest* lie hid,
> Or what strong hand can hold his swift foot back,
> Or who his spoil of beauty can forbid?

The connexion of ideas points naturally to Time *stealing* away the jewel, which is further confirmed by the expression " *Spoil* of Beauty."

The line should be read—

> Where, alack,
> Shall Time's best jewel from Time's *theft* lie hid?

The similarity of type as then used easily accounts for the mistake.

CONTENTS.

	PAGE
HISTORIES—	
King John	9
Richard II	18
1 Henry IV	21
2 Henry IV	24
Henry V	28
1 Henry VI	38
2 Henry VI	40
3 Henry VI	41
Henry VIII	44
TRAGEDIES—	
Troilus and Cressida	45
Coriolanus	58
Titus Andronicus	65
Romeo and Juliet	67
Timon of Athens	71
Julius Cæsar	75
Macbeth	78
Hamlet	82
King Lear	88
Othello	92
Antony and Cleopatra	96
Cymbeline	103

CRITICAL NOTES ON SHAKSPERE'S HISTORIES AND TRAGEDIES.

HISTORIES.

KING JOHN.

Act ii, scene i, line 143—

> It lies as sightly on the back of him
> As great Alcides' shoes upon an *ass:*
> But, Ass, I'll take that burden from your back
> Or lay on that shall make your shoulders crack.

A favourite proverb in Shakspere's age to betoken incongruity was "The shoe of Hercules on a child's foot." So Hooker, Book iv, chapter ix, "The name of blasphemy in this place is like the shoe of Hercules on a child's foot"; where Keble's note, page 445, is "Herculis cothurnos aptare infanti," &c.

The corresponding proverb for fitness, and

aptitude, was in equally common use, "Dignum patinâ operculum."

The application of the proverb in the present instance is so obvious that it naturally leads to a correction of the word "Asse," to make it apposite. "Asse," I apprehend, is nothing but a mistake for "Ape," a still more diminutive creature than a "child," and therefore still more insulting in its employment.

Such a juxtaposition we find in *Much Ado*, v, i, 193, "He is then a giant to an *ape*." And again a "child" compared to an "ape" in *Richard III*, Act iii, i, 130—

>Because that I am little like an *ape*,
>He thinks that you should bear me on your shoulders.

I would therefore propose—

>It lies as sightly on the back of him
>As great Alcides' shoes upon an *ape;*
>But, Ass, I'll take that burden from your back
>Or lay on that shall make your shoulders crack.

Act ii, scene i, line 149—

>*King Lewis*, determine what we shall do straight.
>LEW. Women and fools break off your conference,
>King John, this is the very sum of all :
>England and Ireland, Angiers, Touraine, Maine,
>In right of Arthur do I claim of thee.

That this speech does not belong to Lewis, but to his father, is clear, I think, from the tone of it, "King John, I claim of thee," and from John's answer, "I do defy thee, France"; which words show that it is the two Kings are speaking, and reasonably support Theobald's proposal to give the speech to the "King." The Cambridge Editors' objection to this on the ground that he is uniformly in this scene designated "Fran." or "Fra." overlooks the earlier portion where he is uniformly marked as "King," lines 37, 50, 79.

If the words King and Lew. be simply transposed to mark the speakers, we might alter "Lewis" in the verse to "Let us," reading—

>   LEW. *Let us* determine what we shall do straight.
>   KING. Women and fools break off your conference.

Act ii, scene i, line 354—

> And now he feasts *mousing* the flesh of men,

"Mousing" can hardly be the word. In *Macbeth*, ii, 4, line 13, it is applied to an "owl," as we apply it to a "cat," which seems unworthy of "Death." Pope's emendation "mouthing," interpreted by *Hamlet*, iv, 2, 18, is equally foreign to the purpose, as it goes no further than taking or holding in the

mouth. But "chops," "fangs," and "teeth," point to "mounching."
I would read—

"And now he feasts *mounching* the flesh of men."

Act iii, scene 3, line 37—

> if the midnight bell
> Did, with his iron tongue and brazen mouth,
> Sound on into the drowsy *race* of night.

"Tongue" and "mouth" give reasonable support to the obvious conjecture of "ear," offered by Walker and adopted by Dyce.

"Sound on" will then mean repeating the sounds, in the same way that "Speak on" signifies "continue speaking," as *e.g.*, in *Henry VIII*, Act iii, scene 2, line 306.

"Race," however, suggests the less obvious word "vast" as a nearer emendation. It is used in *Hamlet*, i, 2, 198—

> In the dead *vast* and middle of the night;

and in *Tempest*, i, 2, 327—

> the *vast* of night

and this will yield a finer image of the bell sounding

its strokes into vacancy, and better account for the words "sound on into" suggestive of the sound being lost in the distance.

Act iii, scene 3, line 52—

> Then in despight of *brooded* watchful day.

I imagine the explanation of "brooded," in the sense of "brooding" drawn from vigilance of a hen over her chickens, will hardly be admitted.

Pope's conjecture "broad-eyed" derives some support from *Henry V*, Act ii, 2, 55, "how shall we stretch our eye" as opposed to "winking," and has a natural connexion with our familiar expression "broad daylight."

But this in its ordinary acceptation is strictly confined to the sunrise, which is one objection, and the boldness of the conjecture is another.

King John has already spoken of "Proud day" in line 34 as an hindrance to his divulging his murderous intention, and may be only repeating it here, in which case we should read—

> "Then in despight of *proud and* watchful day."

Act iii, scene 4, line 2—

> "A whole armado of *convicted* sail."

None of the conjectures to correct this unmeaning phrase are entirely satisfactory, as there is no special reason for preferring any one of them to any other, "collected," "connected," "consorted," "combined."

From a somewhat parallel passage in *Othello*, i, 3, 33—

> The Ottomites, reverend and gracious,
> Steering with due course toward the isle of Rhodes,
> Have there *injointed* them with an after fleet,

and from "unjointed" in 1 *Henry IV*, i, 3, 65, and "disjoint" in *Macbeth*, iii, 2, 16, we may probably infer the word is "conjointed," the more so as it is immediately followed by its opposite "disjoined." I would therefore correct—

> "A whole armado of *conjointed* sail."

Act iii, scene 4, line 63—

> Where but by chance a silver drop *hath* fallen,
> Even to that drop ten thousand wiry friends
> Do glue themselves in sociable grief.

The king apparently intimates that Constance's hair had turned suddenly grey with grief. Before, there had been here and there a silver drop, but now "ten thousand wiry friends" are added to it.

This is rendered, to say the least, very obscure

by the employment of the present-perfect "hath";
and as "hath" and "had" are frequently confounded
in print, as, *e.g.*, 2 *Henry VI*, Act i, 1, 88, the sense
becomes much clearer by the pluperfect. I would
therefore read—

> Where but by chance a silver drop *had* fallen,
> Even to that drop ten thousand wiry friends
> Do glue themselves in sociable grief.

Act v, scene 2, line 64—

> LEWIS. And even then, methinks, an angel spake.
> Enter PANDULPH.
> Look where the holy legate comes apace,
> To give us warrant from the hand of heaven,
> And on our actions set the name of right,
> With holy breath.

I can hardly be persuaded to admit the Cambridge
Editors' suggested explanation of the first line, as a
jocose *aside*, connecting "angel" with "purse"
and "noble." It seems entirely out of place in
Lewis's mouth; but after the pathetic expressions
of grief given forth by Salisbury, it would not be
unsuitable to him. He sees the legate coming to
give the English nobles "warrant from the hand of
heaven," and "set the name of right with holy
breath" upon their revolt; and the opportune coin-
cidence of his approach with Lewis's assurances,

warms him to declare that Lewis had spoken like an angel in the words of comfort he had uttered.

I would accordingly propose—

Enter PANDULPH.

SALISBURY.   And even there, methinks, an angel spake [to Lewis];
Look where the holy legate comes apace,
To give us warrant from the hand of heaven,
And on our actions set the name of right,
With holy breath.

Act v, scene 2, line 103—

Have I not heard these islanders shout out
Vive le Roy, as I have *banked* their towns?

The explanation of "banked their towns" as if it were "thrown up entrenchments," or "cast a bank against them," as in Isaiah xxxvii, 33, is alike contrary to the idea of the expedition of the march, and the alacrity of the inhabitants to accept relief from the dominion of their native king.

It may be more plausibly interpreted "Come by sea to the banks on which their towns stood," as "bank" is used in connexion with the "sea," as well as "rivers." See *Merchant of Venice*, v, i, 11; *Othello*, iv, 1, 131.

But as he is apparently speaking of his march, and "banking their towns" would in either case be a very forced expression, I would suggest "*warned*," in the sense of "summon," as it seems to be used in *Julius Cæsar*, v, 1, 5—

> "They mean to *warn* us in Philippi here,"

and read—

> "Have I not heard these islanders shout out
> Vive le Roy, as I have *warned* their towns?"

RICHARD II.

Act ii, scene 2, line 148—

> Farewell at once, *for once, for all*, and ever.

The words "for all" standing separate by a comma are meaningless. "Once for all" is a common turn of expression, for "semel in perpetuum," as in Ainsworth's Latin dictionary s.v., and will suit here well—

> Farewell at once, *for once for all*, and ever.

Act iv, scene 1, line 52 (from the 1st quarto)—

> "I *task the earth* to the like, forsworn Aumerle."

Dr. Johnson proposes "oath" for "earth" in this unintelligible expression, and reads "I *take thy oath*": but the sense seems to require "I take my oath to the like," viz., to Aumerle's being guilty of Gloucester's death: the connexion of the passage shows something like this must be intended.

But the forcible asseveration then in use "I take it on my *death*," makes it more probable that "earth" is a corruption of "death." It is constant in Shakspere and elsewhere.

E.g., King John, i, 1, 110—

> Upon his death-bed he by will bequeathed
> His lands to me, and *took it on his death*
> That this my mother's son was none of his;

where Steevens mistakes the meaning, explaining it "Entertained it as his fixed opinion *when he was dying*,"—a useless repetition, as "on his death-bed" has already occurred. Again, 1 *Henry IV*, Act v, 4, 148, "I'll *take it on my death* I gave him this wound in the thigh."

We may suppose that this form of adjuration took its rise from the imprecation in case of falsehood, which has been rendered notorious by the story on Devizes Market Cross, where the woman begged God to "strike her dead" if she told a lie, and fell a corpse after uttering the words.

The formula "take it on my death," was apparently abbreviated to "take my death," in which form it is found in Latimer's Sermons (page 163, Parker Society): "The first man when he was on the ladder denied the matter utterly, and '*took his death*' upon it, that he never consented to the robbery of the priest." Again, page 180, "She *took her death* she was guiltless in that thing she suffered for," and this form we find in 2 *Henry VI*, Act ii, 3, 87, "I will *take my death* I never meant him any harm."

In either case, whether "oath" or "death," "the" is alike awkward, and as "death" is a less obvious, and equally close emendation, I would propose—

"I *take my death* to the like."

1 HENRY IV.

Act ii, scene 3, line 57—

And in thy face strange motions have appeared
Such as are seen when men restrain their breath
On some great sudden *hast*. O what portents are these?

The quarto reading "hest" affords no better sense than "haste," with which indeed the epithet "sudden" agrees better.
But I do not imagine Lady Percy is thinking of a "surprise," which, in familiar style, is said to "take the breath away," but rather of a difficulty men hold their breath in cope with in a dogged determination, such as is described in *Henry V*, iii, 1, 15—

Now set the teeth, and stretch the nostril wide,
Hold hard the breath and bend up every spirit
To its full height.

This consideration, together with the redundancy of the line, throws doubt on the word "sudden," which indeed Steevens omitted; and recommends "hazard" for "hast." We find it in 2 *Henry IV*, Act iv, 1, 15—

"That your attempts may overlive the *hazard*."

I would accordingly propose—

> And in thy face strange motions have appeared
> Such as we see when men restrain their breath
> On some great *hazard*. What portents are these?

Act ii, scene 4, line 113—

> Didst thou never see Titan kiss a dish of butter?
> Pitiful-hearted *Titan* that melted at the sweet tale
> of the sun.

The person melting at the sun's sweet tale cannot possibly be Titan, who tells the tale. The second "Titan" is evidently a mistake for another name which will answer the description of "melting," or dissolving under his influence or power.

"Melt" is used below, Act iii, scene 1, line 211, for dissolving in tears—

> Nay, if you *melt*, then she will run mad.

Othello, v, 2, 352—

> Albeit unused to the *melting* mood.

And in a sense bearing closer relation to Falstaff's state in *Hamlet*, i, 2, 129—

> O that this too too solid flesh would *melt*,
> Thaw, and resolve itself.

This ambiguous word, I apprehend, affords the

prince an opportunity for a grotesque classical allusion to "*Niobe*," who is as constant an image of "dissolving" as Titan is of "heat."
E.g., Hamlet, 1, 2, 148—

"Like *Niobe*, all tears."

And *Troilus and Cressida*, v, 10, 19—

"Make wells and *Niobes* of the maids and wives."

Parson Evans in the *Merry Wives*, v, 5, 136, tells Falstaff "his pelly is all putter," and he describes himself there, iii, 5, 102, as "being as subject to heat as butter." And our own experience of that article of consumption in July, explains the humour of the prince, when he describes Falstaff as "Niobe," without our requiring consistency to mythology. I would accordingly read—

"Pitiful-hearted *Niobe* that melted at the sweet tale of the sun."

2 HENRY IV.

Act i, scene 3, line 36—

> Yes, if this present quality of war,
> Indeed the instant action : a cause on foot,
> Lives so in hope : As in an early spring,
> We see th' appearing buds, which to prove fruit,
> Hope gives not so much warrant, as despair
> That frosts will bite them.

This passage has been deemed corrupt by almost all editors, Mr. Knight appearing to be the only one to propose no alteration of the words, but to confine it to the punctuation. In this opinion I concur with him, and think all other difficulty of the passage lies in two expressions which have not been perfectly understood, viz., "This present quality of war," and "lives in hope."

As regards the first, Shakspere has a peculiar use of the term "Quality," to which I do not know whether attention has been directed, and which this passage will serve to illustrate.

In our ordinary language now we use it mainly in comparison, as, *e.g.*, we say, "This silk is of inferior quality." We should hardly say, "Silk is of soft quality," or "The quality of silk is soft," speaking of silk in the abstract. We might say, "The quality of silk is softness": but Shakspere, to express this idea, would not scruple to use the adjective, and say "the quality of silk is soft."

Thus, where he writes in *Merchant of Venice*, iv, 1, 179—

> "The *quality* of mercy is not *strained;*"

or, as he might have expressed it, "Mercy is not of a strained quality," he means that it is of the very essence of mercy, an indispensable condition of it, to be unconstrained. Mercy is not mercy if it is not free and voluntary.

So again *Julius Cæsar*, i, 3, 66—

> Why all these things change, from their ordinance,
> Their natures, and pre-formed faculties,
> To *monstrous quality*,

i.e., to quality of monstrousness.

So again in *Julius Cæsar*, iii, 1, 61—

> But I am constant as the northern star,
> Of whose true fixed and *resting quality*
> There is no fellow in the firmament,

i.e., "of its quality of fixedness."

So again *Henry V*, Act v, 2, 18—

> The venom of such looks, we fairly hope,
> Have lost their quality;

which defies grammatical construction, but is nearer our present use—

"Such looks have lost their quality of venom."

Applying this principle to the passage in hand: "This present quality of war," will mean "this war, the quality of which consists in being present, not future," or this war, the essential property, or as logicians speak, the inseparable accident of which is its immediate imminence.

For "present" and "instant" we may compare the language with Act iv, 1, 82—

> The examples
> Of every minute's *instance, present* now,

and *Troilus and Cressida*, iii, 3, 153—

"Take the *instant* way."

As regards the other phrase, "lives in hope," it is, I apprehend, nothing but the colloquialism, "I live in hope," for " I entertain," or "indulge in, the hope."

Thus understanding these two expressions, although the construction is somewhat involved, the sense of the whole is clear enough. Lord Bardolph urging compromise when it is possible, declares that a time when we are called upon to put all to an immediate issue, when the action is imminent, when the cause is afoot, is not a time to indulge in hopes of any future, remote, and problematical contingency, which may prove as illusory as the promise of a too early Spring.

"Instant action," "cause on foot," are, in fact, explanatory of, and in apposition to, "present quality;" and we may read—

> Yes, if this present quality of war—
> Indeed, the instant action—a cause on foot,
> Lives so in hope, as in an early spring
> We see th' appearing buds; which to prove fruit
> Hope gives not so much warrant, as despair
> That frosts will bite them.

HENRY V.

Act i, scene 1, line 47—

> When he speaks
> The air, a chartered libertine, is still,
> And *the mute wonder* lurketh in men's ears
> To steal his sweet and honeyed sentences.

"The mute wonder" cannot be an allowable expression if "mute" be supposed the attribute of wonder. "The" is indeed found before certain abstract nouns, as "The wars," "The vengeance," "The policy," "The spoil"; but it cannot be used indefinitely here, as if "the mute wonder" meant "mute wonder."

There is indeed a somewhat similar turn in *Richard II*, Act i, 2, 58—

> Grief boundeth where it falls,
> Not with *the* empty hollowness, but weight:

which may perhaps be defended as if it meant "not with the empty hollowness of a ball;" but the unusual place of the definite article suggests the possessive pronoun as preferable "not with *his* empty hollowness, but weight."

Anyhow, in the present instance, the solecism is easily removed by a comma. As the "air" is a "libertine," so "wonder" is a "mute" in the sense in which we find it in *Hamlet*, v, 2, 322—

> You that look pale and tremble at this chance,
> That are but *mutes and audience* to this act.

I would therefore read—

> And *the mute*, Wonder, lurketh in men's ears
> To steal his sweet and honeyed sentences.

Act i, scene 2, line 93—

> And rather choose to hide them in a net
> Than amply to *imbar* their crooked title.

I am surprised that the word "amply" has not suggested "unvaile" (to use Cotgrave's spelling) for "imbarre," for which there is the support of *Twelfth Night*, i, 1, 27—

> The element itself, till seven years' heat,
> Shall not behold her face at *ample* view;
> But, like a cloistress, she will *veiled* walk.

But Theobald's conjecture "unbare," adopted by Capell, affords an opportunity for the consideration of the prefix "un," which may at the same time support his emendation here and illustrate other passages.

Miss Baker, in her Glossary of Northamptonshire Words, has the following article, "Abate: to make bare; to uncover; to clear away or remove the superincumbent soil preparatory to working stone in a quarry. Bate, onbare, *unbare*, and unbate are all cognate terms (*i.e.*, synonymous). Uncallow is correspondent in East Anglia."

Again, "Ungive: to begin to thaw; gingerbread losing its crispness, and salt, or any other substance relaxing from the humidity of the atmosphere, are said to ungive. Give, forgive, ongive, are similarly applied." I can bear testimony to the constant use of "ongiving" as applied to the weather, or soil, after a frost.

Shakspere certainly so uses "unloose" uniformly in the sense of "loose," as, *e.g.*, in this play, Act i, scene 1, line 46—

> The Gordian knot of it he will *unloose*
> Familiar as his garter.

Again, *Lear*, ii, 2, 69—

> "bite the holy cords a-twain
> Which are too intrinse to *unloose*."

These, I think, support Theobald's conjecture "unbare."

I think too it will go far to support Mr. Beckett's

conjecture on the difficult passage in *Othello*, Act iv, scene 2, line 54—

> but, alas! to make me
> A fixed figure for the time of scorn
> To point his slow *unmoving* finger at.

He would read "slow-unmoving," I suppose, in the sense of "slow-moving." Time is slow to take his finger *off* or away, and thus "unmoving," by the analogy of "unloosing," will signify *re*moving.

Dr. Farmer seems, in his note on the words in *Measure for Measure*, v, 1, 166, "In this I'll be *im*partial," to prove a similar peculiarity with regard to the prefix "*im*," "impartial" being there used for "partial." And this will possibly account for "*im*perseverant," in *Cymbeline*, iv, 1, 13, where "obstinate" is apparently the sense required, as we find the terms connected in *Hamlet*, i, 2, 92, "to persevere in obstinate condolement."

Act iv, scene 1, line 230—

> What? is thy *soul* of *Odoration*?

This is corrected by Mr. Knight—

> "What is thy soul of adoration?"

"Adoration" was given in the second folio, but

"thy soul of adoration" is a very awkward turn if by it he meant the soul or innermost principle of the adoration ceremony offers. Nor do any of the other conjectures remove the difficulty.

The king has been asking ceremony to show him its "worth," *i.e.*, all it was worth in "rents" and "comings in," as we speak of a person being "worth" so much, meaning "possessing" it. He may naturally be supposed to add in the same vein, "What is the *sum* total of the adoration which belongs to you?" and this without force may be shortened into "What is thy sum of adoration?" as we have a similar use of "thy sum" in *As You Like It*, ii, 1, 48—

>   Giving thy *sum* of more
>   To that which had too much.

I would accordingly propose—

>   "What is thy *sum* of *Adoration?*"

Act iv, scene 1, line 275—

>   Take from them now
>   The sense of reckoning *of* the opposed numbers:
>   Pluck their hearts from them.

Steevens, after Tyrwhitt's conjecture, has changed "of" to "if," and his reading is adopted by the

Cambridge Editors, not, however, without misgiving, as their note shows, in which they suspect the omission of a line.

The prayer as the author first wrote it in the quarto—

> Take from them now the sense of reckoning,
> *That* the opposed multitudes which stand before them
> May not appall their courage,

is so eminently beautiful, begging the skill of calculation to be effaced from the soldiers' minds, that I can hardly conceive Shakspere would weaken its force in any subsequent alteration of the place. This, to my mind, is conclusive against "if," by which the prayer is made hypothetical.

Theobald's emendation "lest" preserves the simplicity of the prayer in a greater degree. The objection to it is its divergence from the letter of the text.

The same objection holds against "ere," which else would suit, as we find it similarly used in a form of request in *Cymbeline*, iii, 4, 9—

> put thyself
> Into a humour of less fear, *ere* wildness
> Vanquish my staider senses.

But the objection will not stand against "or," which the Cambridge Editors record as an anonymous conjecture, and which requires nothing but the change of a letter.

The use of " or " for " ere " is well known in older English, *e.g.*, in Latimer's Sermons, page 201, Parker: " Ye may chance to be caught *or* ye go." Dr. Abbott indeed, section 131, allows only of the combination of the two words in Shakspere, " or ere." But I think there are proofs of its simple use in several places.

E.g., in *Hamlet*, v, 2, 30, where the folio reads—

> "*Ere* I could make a prologue to my brains
> They had begun the play,"

the quarto reads—

> "*Or* I could make a prologue "

Again, I conceive it is so used in *Richard II*, Act i, 1, 78—

> By that and all the rites of knighthood else,
> Will I make good against thee, arm to arm
> What I have spoke, *or* thou canst worse devise,

i.e., and so put a stop to thy further treasonable machinations.

Again, taken too in this sense, it gives greater force to Cranmer's prayer in *Henry VIII*, Act v, 1, 140—

> God and your majesty
> Protect mine innocence, *or* I fall into
> The trap is laid for me,

which turn of expression lends great support to a similar reading of the text—

> Take from them now
> The sense of reckoning, *or* the opposed numbers
> Pluck their heart from them.

Before leaving the subject I would take occasion to remark on an elliptical use of the conjunction "or," which is equally unnoticed by Dr. Abbott in his valuable Grammar, though of frequent occurrence in Shakspere. The present play affords several instances.

Act iii, scene 1, line 1—

> Once more unto the breach, dear friends, once more ;
> *Or* close the wall up with our English dead,

which means apparently, "up again to the breach, *even if* we have to fill it up with our corpses."

Again, Act iii, scene 2, line 109—

> Ay'll do gud service, *or* ay'll lig i' the ground for it,

i.e., *even* if I die for it.

Again, Act iv, scene 3, line 116—

> And my poor soldiers tell me, yet ere night
> They'll be in fresher robes, *or* they will pluck
> The gay new coats o'er the French soldiers' heads,
> And turn them out of service,

which may mean equally "*even* if they have to strip the French soldiers of them."

Thus again, 2 *Henry IV*, Act ii, scene 2, line 108—

> "Nay, they will be kin to us, *or* they will fetch it from Japhet,"

i.e., even if they have to trace their pedigree through the remote common ancestor of Scripture.

In all these instances the ellipse is to be supplied by the alternative understood, to which the conjunction corresponds. "Up to the breach, and *either* conquer *or* die." "I'll do good service, and *either* vanquish or *die*." "My poor soldiers will be in fresher robes, *either* arrayed in immortal vesture *or* in the Frenchmen's coats." "They will claim kindred *either* in a closer degree, *or* by our common relationship to Japhet."

Act iv, scene 3, line 49—

> Old men forget ; *yet all shall* be forgot,
> *But* he'll remember with advantages
> What feats he did this day.

The meaning required is clear enough, viz., that, however treacherous the old men's memory may become, yet their actions done that day would not escape them. This, which cannot be extracted from the words as they stand, is easily derived from their simple transposition—

> Old men forget ; *but, shall all* be forgot,
> *Yet* he'll remember with advantages
> What feats he did this day.

We should perhaps say, "*Should* all be forgot ;" but "shall all" corresponding to "he'll remember," is equally allowable and more grammatical.

1 HENRY VI.

Act i, scene 1, line 55—

> A far more glorious star thy soul shall make
> Than Julius Cæsar, or bright . . . .

Conjectures to fill the line up have been mostly of constellations which owe their origin to apotheosis, so as to correspond to Julius Cæsar. To this purpose Berenice, Cassiopeia, Orion, and Cepheus have been enlisted in the cause; but as brilliancy seems principally intended, it would be natural to suppose Venus to be the star designed as we find below, scene 2, line 143, "*Bright* Star of Venus," which under its other name of "Hesperus" will suit the metre—

> A far more glorious star thy soul shall make
> Than Julius Cæsar, or bright *Hesperus*.

Act i, scene 1, line 76—

> "A third thinks without expense at all."

"One," "another," "a third," follow in such order, that rather than supply "man," as is done by the later folios, I would keep "a third" to its place, and add "he," as is done in other instances, *e.g.*, *Cymbeline*, i, 1, 40, "The King, he takes the babe."

"A third, *he* thinks without expense at all."

Act iv, scene 1, line 102—

"For though he seem with forged quaint conceit
To set a gloss upon his *bold* intent."

As we have "bad intent" in *Measure for Measure*, v, 1, 449; "ill intent," *Pericles*, iv, 6, 103; "good intents," 2 *Henry IV*, Act v, 2, 143; and as here his "setting a gloss" upon his intent shews it is malice rather than boldness that is in question, I would read—

"To set a gloss upon his *bad* intent."

2 HENRY VI.

Act iv, scene 8, line 44—

> "Crying *Villiago!* unto all they meet."

Perhaps the account of a French invasion in *King John*, v, 2, 103—

> Have I not heard these islanders shout out
> *Vive le roy?*

may justify the conjecture that it is the same cry here of which *Villiago* is the distorted representation.

3 HENRY VI.

Act i, scene 1, line 267—

> Whose haughty spirit, winged with desire,
> Will *cost* my crown, and, like an empty eagle,
> Tire on the flesh of me and of my sons.

"Crest" is used for "surmount," or, "take place of advantage over," in *Antony and Cleopatra*, v, 2, 82—

> his reared arm
> *Crested* the world.

And Salisbury in *King John*, iv, 3, 45, describes the infamy of Arthur's supposed murder as—

> "the very top,
> The height, the *crest* or crest unto the *crest*
> Of murder's arms."

And this has given rise, I suppose, to our modern expressions, "Crest the hill," or "Crest the wave."

It is connected with "Crown," in *Midsummer Night's Dream*, iii, 2, 214—

> "*Crowned* with one *crest*,"

and this favours the idea of a similar reversed juxtaposition in the text—

> Whose haughty spirit, winged with desire
> Will *crest* my crown.

The objection to this change is that some term of falconry is supposed to be more natural—in accordance with which Hanmer read "truss," which he explains (see note in Cambridge Edition) of "seizing in the air," as a "hawk does a fowl." But "winged with desire" is so patent an attribute of a "haughty spirit," or "aspiring" mind as, *e.g.*, in Ken's morning hymn—

> "Had I your wings to heaven I'd fly,
> But God shall that defect supply,
> And my soul *winged* with warm *desire*,
> Shall all day long to heaven *aspire*,"

that it may be regarded simply as descriptive of ambition, and have no further reference to an "empty eagle," than as it gave the author occasion of introducing the simile, after he had employed the metaphor.

I would accordingly propose—

> "Whose haughty spirit, winged with desire
> Will *crest* my crown : and, like an empty eagle,
> Tire on the flesh of me, and of my sons."

Act ii, scene 6, line 100—

"For *in* thy shoulder do I build my seat."

The other folios read "on thy shoulder," which must, I think, be right, as the phrase "build on the back" is elsewhere found, as in Hooker's Preface, page 195, Edition Keble: "*On* our backs they also build that are lewd," though there it is a literal translation from Greg. Nazianzen.

HENRY VIII.

Act ii, scene 4, line 111—

> You have, by fortune and his highness' favours,
> Gone slightly o'er low steps, and now are mounted
> Where *Powers* are your retainers, and *your words*,
> Domestics to you, serve your will as't please
> Yourself pronounce their office.

"Powers" can only, I imagine, refer to the highest Potentates, Kings, and Emperors; and the Queen can hardly mean to imply that her husband and her uncle were the Cardinal's *retainers*.

In Act iii, scene 2, line 410, Wolsey says about himself—

> No sun shall ever usher forth mine honours,
> Or gild again the *noble troops* that waited
> Upon my smiles.

Mason proposed "our lords" for "your words," and if the further correction of "Powers" to "Peers" be made, it will give a sense to the Queen's reproach, in keeping with his boast—

> "Where *Peers* are your retainers, and *our Lords*,
> Domestics to you, serve your will, as't please
> Yourself pronounce their office."

TRAGEDIES.

TROILUS AND CRESSIDA.

Act i, scene 2, line 7—

>And like as there were husbandry in war,
>Before the sun rose he was harnessed *lyte*.

"Lyte," I apprehend, is nothing but a mistake for " early."

In *Romeo and Juliet*, i, 1, 116—

>Madam, an hour *before the worshipped sun
>Peered forth* the golden window of the East.
>* * * * *
>So *early* walking did I see your son.

And the connexion of early rising with thrift and good housekeeping is obvious. We find it in *Henry V*, Act iv, scene 1, line 6—

>For our bad neighbour makes us *early* stirrers,
>Which is both healthful and good *husbandry*.

Act i, scene 3, line 51—

>"And flies *fled* under shade."

"Fled" is more likely to be a mistake for "fleet" —the form in which Shakspere uniformly employs the word otherwise spelt "flit," than an elliptical phrase, as Dr. Abbott explains it, supposing "are" understood.

Act i, scene 3, line 59—

> Besides the applause and approbation
> The which, most mighty for thy place and sway,
> And thou most reverend for thy stretched-out life,
> I give to both your speeches : which were such
> As Agamemnon *and the hand* of Greece
> Should hold up high in brass : and such again
> As venerable Nestor (hatched in silver)
> Should with a bond of air, strong as the axletree
> On which the heavens ride, knit all Greekes ears
> To *his* experienced tongue : yet let it please both
> Thou great, and wise, to hear Ulysses speak.

The mixture of second and third persons is so arbitrary, and produces so much confusion, that scarce any sense can be made of this passage. To read the whole in the second by altering "his" to "thy," with the further change of "all the hands" for "and the hand," to correspond to "all the ears," of line 67, will give an intelligible meaning.

> Besides the applause and approbation
> The which, most mighty for thy place and sway,
> And thou most reverend for thy stretched-out life,
> I give to both your speeches which were such

> As, Agamemnon, *all the hands* of Greece
> Should hold up high in brass : and such again
> As, venerable Nestor, hatched in silver,
> Should with a bond of air, strong as the axletree
> On which heaven rides, knit all *the Greekish* ears
> To *thy* experienced tongue :

Act i, scene 3, line 73—

> "When rank Thersites opes his *mastic* jaws."

"Mastiff," Rowe's conjecture, seems too complimentary. I do not see why we should scruple at "nasty," which is so obvious a conjecture, that I can only suppose no editor has ventured on it because it was thought too ignoble an expression for Agamemnon to employ. But he may regard Thersites as a "nastie fellow," as Cotgrave interprets the French word "souillon," and in this relation to his *person* apply it to his "jaws." Pistol makes use of a similar expression, *Henry V*, Act ii, 1, 46, "Within thy nasty mouth." It is in keeping with "rank," which precedes.

Act i, scene 3, line 89—

> And therefore is the glorious planet Sol,
> In noble eminence enthroned and sphered
> Amidst the other : whose medicinable eye
> Corrects the ill aspects of planets evil,

And *posts*, like the commandment of a King,
Sans check, *to* good and bad : but when the planets
In evil mixture to disorder wander, &c.

The corrective power of Sol, who with his "medicinable eye" overrules the "ill aspects of planets evil," and prevents their "evil mixture," may reasonably be said to "*part* the good and bad;" but I cannot understand how an "eye" can "post."

"Sans check" may seem to justify "posts," as signifying the speed of an *unchecked* course; but it is equally applicable to "commandment" alone, signifying without obstacle interposed. In this sense it is found in *King John*, iii, 4, 151—

none so small advantage shall step forth
To *check* his reign, but they will cherish it.

"Part good and bad," for "good from bad," is Shakspere's ordinary turn of expression, as *Love's Labour's Lost*, i, 2, 7, "How canst thou *part* sadness *and* melancholy," and 2 *Henry IV*, Act i, 2, 215, "part young limbs *and* lechery."

What recommends this emendation to my mind, is not only the words "evil mixture" in the following line, but that by means of it we get rid of the confusion caused by the variety of images which is brought in by the word "posts."

I would accordingly suggest—

> Corrects the ill aspects of planets evil,
> And *parts*, like the commandment of a King,
> Sans check, *the* good and bad.

Act i, scene 3, line 238—

> Good arms, strong joints, true swords ; and *Jove's accord*
> Nothing so full of heart.

Steevens explains "Jove's accord" by "Jove probante," whether from "accord" in the sense of "agreement," or "grant," I do not know—a very awkward mode of expression, certainly, and which can hardly be acknowledged admissible.

It seems more likely that Æneas appeals to heaven to witness to his avowal that the Trojans are courageous in their cause; which may recommend "*Jove record*," in the sense of "Jove be witness," in the same way as it is used in Scripture, Phil. i, 8, "God is my record."

Act i, scene 3, line 367—

> What glory our Achilles *shares* from Hector,
> Were he not proud, we all should share with him.

The verse 145 of Act iv, scene 5—

> "A thought of added honour *torn* from Hector,"

may possibly warrant "*tears* from Hector" here.

D

Act iii, scene 1, line 114—

"Yet that which seems the wound to kill."

"Wound" is passive participle for "wounded," like "wed" for "wedded," and should be added to the list of similarly contracted forms given in Dr. Abbott, section 342.

The line answers in sense and metre to 110—

The shaft confounds not that it wounds,

where Dr. Johnson places a comma after "confounds," to the destruction of the sense, reading, according to Pope's division of the verses—

The shaft confounds,
Not that it wounds,
But tickles still the sore.

But how can the shaft confound, if it only tickles? Love's shaft, says the song, is not fatal, it does not overthrow whom it wounds, but causes a half-pleasurable sensation.

Act iii, scene 2, line 21—

death, I fear me,
Sounding *destruction*, or some joy too fine.

In Act v, 2, 41, where the folio reads rightly

"distraction," the quarto has "distruction." I think there can be no doubt they both alike are wrong here, and that we should read—

> death, I fear me,
> Swooning, *distraction*, or some joy too fine.

Act iii, scene 2, line 169—

> "As *plantage to the moon.*"

No satisfactory conjecture has been offered to correct this unmeaning phrase.

Troilus is enumerating the things *proverbial* for truth, and this almost proves, I think, that whatever "Plantage to the moon" stands for must be one of the most noted symbols of constancy.

The moon can therefore hardly find place among the subjects of comparison, as it is the emblem of the contrary, *Romeo and Juliet*, ii, 2, "the inconstant moon." Nothing can we imagine with reference to it betokening constancy, except the tides, which is the ground of Heath's conjecture "Floodage" for "Plantage." If the author had meant this, he might have said, as "ocean to the moon." But the tides are certainly not numbered among proverbs of constancy, as the other similes are.

The North Star, however, is Shakspere's familiar image of constancy, *e.g.*, Julius Cæsar, iii, 1, 60—

> But I am *constant* as the Northern Star,
> Of whose *true* fixed and resting quality
> There is no fellow in the firmament.

It is apparently designated "Pole" in Shakspere and other writers, as it afterwards obtained the title of "Pole Star."

E.g., *Antony and Cleopatra*, iv, 15, 65—

> "The soldiers' *pole* is fallen,"

i.e., the soldiers' guiding star ; for I cannot imagine that "pole" here has any reference to "garland" immediately preceding, "Withered is the garland of the war ;" which would appear the only justification of Dr. Johnson's interpretation of "Pole," as a "pageant held high for observation." "Garland" is the victor's crown, as in *Coriolanus*, Act i, 9, 59—

> Caius Marcius
> Wears this war's *garland*.

Again, it is so used in *Othello*, ii, 1, 15—

> Seems to cast water on the burning bear,
> And quench the guards of the ever-fixed *Pole*.

Again, in *Eastward Hoe*, Act i, scene 1 —("British Drama," vol. 2, p. 85), we read—

> "I knew by the elevation of the *Pole*."

Again, in Habington's *Castara*, p. 143, Edition Arber—

> The wandering Pilot sweats to find
> The causes that produce the wind
> Still gazing on the *Pole*.

These passages warrant us in concluding that "Pole" was used for the North Star, and may dispose us to believe that "*Moon*" in this place is a mistake for "*Pole*," of which fixture, unalterableness, and stability are the characteristics.

This fixture and stability, I conceive, is denoted by the word "Plantage," derived from the word "Plant," constantly used in an analogous sense—as *e.g.*, *Merchant of Venice*, iii, 5, 57—

> The fool hath *planted* in his memory
> An army of good words,

and *Richard II*, Act iv, scene 1, line 127—

> Anointed, crowned, *planted* many years,

a sense derived from the French, as in Cotgrave, "Planter," "to settle, fix, ground." "Plantage," it must be allowed, has a strange sound; but there is no ordinary term I know of to express the idea. "Fixedness" we might perhaps say, for which Shakspere has "fixure" in Act i, 3, 101 ; but this again is equally removed from common use ; while the authority of Scripture, Isaiah li, 16, "that I may *plant* the heavens, and lay the foundation of the earth" gives a reason for the preferable use of *plantage*, if indeed "planting," an English word, be not better.

I would therefore beg to submit, with diffidence, the change I propose—

> As true as steel, as *plantage to the Pole*.

Act iii, scene 3, line 28—

> And he shall buy my daughter ; and her presence
> Shall quite strike off all service I have done,
> In most accepted *pain*.

Hanmer proposed "pay," which, though to the purpose, does not yield quite so good a sense as "gain." Calchas has declared that Antenor shall "buy" his daughter. The exchange he reckons as a *gain*, overbalancing the services he had rendered the Greeks. "Accepted" is of course in the sense of "acceptable ;" see Abbott, section 375.

According to this we should read—

> ' In most accepted *gain*."

Act iii, scene 3, line 110—

> For speculation turns not to itself,
> Till it hath travelled and is *married* there,
> Where it may see itself.

"Speculation," I suppose, is nothing else but "vision," as in *Macbeth*, iii, 4, 95—

> Thou hast no speculation in those eyes.

"Married" seems opposed to the purpose of the passage; for the eyes which meet, and mutually "salute," cannot in that process be said to "marry." On the contrary, the eye, Ulysses says, requires to be separated from itself, by distance, to become by reflection its own object of contemplation.

I should propose in accordance with this—

> For speculation turns not to itself
> Till it have travelled, and is *carried* there
> Where it may see itself.

Act iv, scene 2, line 4—

> Sleep *kill* those pretty eyes,
> And give as soft attachment to thy senses
> As *infants* empty of all thought!

The proximity of *infants* makes it probable that Troilus, in the forced language of lovers, wishes sleep to be like a kind mother, to "lull" her to rest, and thus we should read—

> Sleep *lull* those pretty eyes.

Act v, scene 2, line 169—

> not the dreadful spout
> Which shipmen do the hurricano call,
> Constringed in *mass* by the almighty Feñne.

The quarto reads "Sun," which is generally adopted, possibly from some physical theory of its connection with the waterspout, of which I am ignorant. Otherwise the folio would seem better if we read "Fan" for Fen. So we find in Act i, scene 3, line 27—

> Distinction with a broad and powerful *fan*,
> Puffing at all, *winnows* the light away,
> And what hath *mass*, and matter by itself
> Lies rich in virtue and unmingled.

"Fan" is again used with "wind" below in scene 3, line 41—

> Even in the *fan* and wind of your fair sword.

In modern science, at all events, the waterspout is considered, I believe, to be produced by the contest of two contrary winds, and "constringed in *mass*" falls in well with the passage quoted.

Act v, scene 3, line 26—

"Mine honour keeps the *weather* of my fate."

This passage has been left as it stands by every editor; for Steevens' proposed reading "off" for "of" does not help the meaning in any way that I can discern.

Hector is declaring that he prefers honour to life, that he disregards death or fate in comparison; that honour *stands before* it.

This sense will be obtained if we read—

"Mine honour keeps the *vaward* of my fate."

To "have the vaward" is found in *Midsummer Night's Dream*, iv, 1, 101—

"And since we have the *vaward* of the day."

CORIOLANUS.

Act i, scene 3, line 38—

> The breasts of Hecuba,
> When she did suckle Hector, looked not lovelier
> Than Hector's forehead, when it spit forth blood
> At Grecian sword. *Contenning*, tell Valeria
> We are fit to bid her welcome.

May not this word, awkwardly replaced by either "contending" or "condemning," be a mistake for "Content ye," addressed to Virgilia, or "content thee"? Such a phrase is constant in Shakspere to bespeak acquiescence, as, *e.g.*, *Troilus and Cressida*, iii, 2, 135, "Pray you, *content you*," as it is found, too, in Scripture, 2 Kings v, 23, "Be content, take two talents." Here it expresses Volumnia's desire that Virgilia will allow of Valeria's visit, and turning to the Gentleman, she bids her to be admitted.

Act i, scene 5, line 23—

> Thy friend no less
> Than *those* she placeth highest!

There are many passages in Shakspere which

seem to indicate that he used "those" for a genitive plural, as "their" or "theirs," which use in these places might be marked by an apostrophe, "those'."

This has not been observed by Dr. Abbott in his account of his pronouns; but deserves, I think, consideration as affording an easy solution of constructions otherwise exceedingly irregular.

E.g., Act ii, scene 2, line 23, " His ascent is not by such easy degrees as those, who," &c., *i.e.*, as "theirs, who."
Again, *Richard III*, Act i, scene 3, line 217—

> If heaven have any grievous plagues in store
> Exceeding *those* that I can wish on thee,

i.e., exceeding "theirs," the plagues, viz., which she had been imprecating on the others, which might seem to have exhausted her power of cursing, and the lines should be read—

> If heaven have any grievous plagues in store
> Exceeding *those'* that I can wish on thee.

In *Merchant of Venice*, Act i, 1, 97—

> when, I am very sure,
> If they should speak, would almost damn *those ears*,
> *Which* hearing them would call their brothers fools.

And in *Henry VIII*, Act ii, scene i, line 151—

> He sent command to the Lord Mayor straight,
> To stop the rumour and allay *those tongues*
> *That* durst disperse it.

"Those ears," and "those tongues," may mean "those hearers," and "those speakers," as in French they call a person a "mauvaise langue" who speaks evil of others. But it will be scarcely possible to understand on the same principle—

> *Pericles*, i, 4, 39, "*Those* palates, *who*,"
> and i, 4, 34, "*These* mouths, *whom*."

Act i, scene 9, line 45—

> When steel grows soft as the parasite's silk,
> Let *him* be made an overture for the wars.

Steevens and Malone assert in their note that "him" is not unfrequently used by our author, and other writers of his age, instead of "it." As regards our author, Dr. Abbott makes no mention of it, which he would have done if he had observed it.

"Overture" is so naturally connected with "war" that the error lies much more probably in "him," which may very likely be a mistake for some word indicative of the behaviour of the parasite, as distinguished from the warrior.

"Smiles" are the mark of the courtier, as in *Love's Labour's Lost*, v, 2, 331—

> "'This is the flower that *smiles* on every one,"

and of the parasite in line 464—

> some *trencher knight*, some Dick
> That *smiles* his cheek in years.

I would accordingly suggest with diffidence—

> When steel grows soft as the parasite's silk,
> Let *smiles* be made an overture for the wars.

Act ii, scene 1, line 49—

> "Meeting two such wealsmen as you are (I cannot call you Lycurgusses), if the drink you give me touch my palate adversely, I make a crooked face at it."

This passage has been left without alteration by the editors, when the suppression of the parenthesis is, I think, evidently demanded by the sense. Menenius is piquing himself on his frankness, and declares that he cannot call such politicians as these Lycurgusses on any occasion when he falls in with them. I think it clear we should read—

> "Meeting two such wealsmen as you are, I cannot call you Lycurgusses. If the drink you give me touch my palate adversely, I make a crooked face at it."

Act ii, scene 2, line 107—

> alone he enter'd
> The mortal gate of the city, which he *painted*
> With shunless destiny.

As the author calls Coriolanus's sword " Death's stamp," I can hardly conceive he would so soon change his metaphor and speak of his "*painting*" the gate with death ; but he may more consistently be said to have *printed* it with ruin, as he left on it the *mark* of inevitable fate.

We may compare *Titus Andronicus*, iii, 1, 170—

> *Writing* destruction on the enemies castle.

Act iii, scene 1, line 89—

> Shall remain !
> Hear you this Triton of the minnows ? Mark you
> His absolute " shall "?
> COM. 'Twas from the canon.
> COR. " Shall " !

If Cominius interrupts the speech with the words " 'Twas from the Canon," they can only mean, as Mason paraphrases, " it was according to law." But such a declaration is little calculated to assuage Coriolanus's violence, and the meaning of " canon " in all other places is " Divine law," the language of the Ten Commandments, " Thou shalt " and

"Thou shalt not," so *All's Well*, i, 1, 136, "The most inhibited sin in the *canon*." See also *King John*, ii, 1, 179—

> Thy sins are visited in this poor child,
> The *canon* of the law is laid on him.

See also *Hamlet*, i, 2, 131—

> Or that the Everlasting had not fixed
> His *canon* 'gainst self-slaughter!

The imperious "shall," Coriolanus might naturally declare, belonged to a law with heavenly sanction, not to mortal voice; and the force of the term will be preserved if we continue the speech to him without interruption—

His absolute "shall,"—'Twas from the canon, "Shall"!

Act iii, scene 2, line 72—

> I prithee now, my son,
> Go to them with this bonnet in thy hand,
> And thus far having stretched it (*here be with* them),
> Thy knee bussing the stones.

"Here be with them" is, I suppose, unintelligible and can derive no explanation from the following words, "thy knee bussing the stones," which clearly refer to the "courtesy" he should make the people at the same time that he held his bonnet low. It may readily be corrected to "*bewitch* them" in accordance with Act ii, 3, 94, "I will counterfeit the *bewitchment* of some popular man," in which case "here" must be changed to "there," *i.e.*, when he is before the people.

Possibly a line may have dropped out, which might be supplied from the parallel passage in *Richard II*, Act i, 4, 26—

> there *bewitch* them
> *With humble and familiar courtesy,*
> Thy knee bussing the stones ;

but sense is made even without the supplemental line by the change proposed—

> "*there bewitch them,*
> Thy knee bussing the stones."

Act iii, scene 3, line 25—

> he hath been used
> Ever to conquer, and to have his worth
> *Of* contradiction.

If we change "of contradiction" to "'bove contradiction," the sense is clear. He has always been accustomed to have his worth regarded so highly, such deference paid him, that he has never been contradicted.

TITUS ANDRONICUS.

Act ii, scene 3, line 126—

And with that painted *hope* braves your mightiness.

Demetrius implies that Lavinia's chastity and loyalty were affected, which may have been expressed by "show," and the following word "she" had been inadvertently omitted by the printers.
The line would then run—

And with that painted *show she* braves your mightiness.

Act iii, scene 2, line 61—

How would he hang his slender gilded wings,
And buzz lamenting *doings* in the air.

" Buzz lamenting doings " is unintelligible.
The text in this play is so correct that a wide departure from it lies under strong prejudice, or else "dirges" on the occasion of his son's death might be deemed a fitting occupation for the parent fly. "Lamenting dolings," as proposed by Theobald, seems but a weak repetition.
Perhaps the author wrote "lamenting *goings*." The parent fly droops his wings and *goes* to and

fro in the air buzzing his lamentations. To "buzz lamenting *goings*" will then mean gives his movement lamentable sound, and thus virtually sound and motion become one.

This, though audacious, is not foreign to Shakspere's practice. We have a similar union of two distinct senses in *Twelfth Night*, i, 1, 5, where he paraphrases the "zephyr," by the complex idea of fragrance and sound together, calling it "sweet sound." "Goings" is a Scriptural term, as in Psalm xvii, 5, "O hold thou up my 'goings' in thy paths," and is used for "walking" in *Lear*, iii, 2, 94, "*Going* shall be used with feet." And whatever our translators understood by the words, they have made the same union of sound and motion in the well-known verse 2 Samuel, v, 24, "When thou hearest a *sound of a going* in the tops of the mulberry trees."

ROMEO AND JULIET.

Act i, scene 1, line 183—

> Why, *such is love's* trangression.
> Griefs of my own lie heavy in my breast;
> Which thou wilt propagate, to have it prest
> With more of thine.

Romeo declares that his friend's compassion for his distress, so far from removing it, increases it by the sense that he is the cause of sorrow in another—

> This *love* that thou hast shown,
> Doth add more grief to too much of my own.

Such an effect of sympathy he styles "love's transgression" as contradicting its purpose, which is by sharing sorrow to take part away. But this cannot be made out of the short and unsatisfactory line—

> "Why, such is love's trangression."

But I think it is likely that in the constant course of repetition, the word "love" has slipped out here, and that we should read—

> "Why, such *a love* is love's transgression."

Act i, scene 3, line 2—

> Now, by my maidenhead, at twelve years old I *bad* her come. What, lamb! what, ladybird! God forbid! Where's this girl? what, Juliet!

The nurse, I conceive, deprecates the authority which Lady Capulet gives her in the words "call her forth to me," and replies, "Does it become me to *bid* her come, as if she were a child, and she now a woman, twelve years old and more. God forbid!" Accordingly she employs first endearing titles, "lamb" and "ladybird," but, losing patience, *bids* her in the familiar style, "Where's this girl! What, Juliet!" This may justify "bid" for "bad." I do not think we need stumble at the nurse's adjuration, "Now, by my maidenhead," which may be in her mouth nothing but a strong expression for truth used unreflectingly; as we find "by my troth and maidenhead," *Henry VIII*, Act ii, 3, 23. I would accordingly suggest—

NURSE. Now, by my maidenhead, at twelve years old I *bid* her come! What, lamb! What, ladybird! God forbid!——Where's this girl? What, Juliet!

Act iii, scene 2, line 5—

> Spread thy close curtain, love-performing night,
> That *runaways* eyes may wink and Romeo
> Leap to these arms untalked of and unseen.

There will be no difficulty here if "runaways" can mean spies, or tell-tales, which the words "untalked of, and unseen," naturally suggest, and I think demand.

In support of such a meaning attaching to "runaway," which has appeared so arbitrary that the word has given rise to a multitude of conjectures, I think we may quote the familiar expression, "don't run away with the idea," as it is used with regard to belief on insufficient evidence. Similarly we say, "They ran away with the story"; which brings the sense closer to that required in the text, as it implies their hurry to retail it.

Besides this indirect proof derived from common language, I think it is used in the same sense in *Merchant of Venice*, ii, 6, 47—

"For the *close* night doth play the *runaway*."

"Play the runaway" can hardly mean that the night was passing away, at nine o'clock. Besides, if this were intended we should rather expect "quick" or "short" than "close." "*Play the* eavesdropper" is a phrase given in Cotgrave. Lorenzo hastens Jessica by telling her that the darkness of the night exposed them to being overheard. This he might fairly express by saying that "the close night played the eavesdropper." Juliet desires "*close*" night that none may "spy." Whether "spy" or "eavesdropper," they would be equally "telltales," which may be the sense of "runaway" in both places.

I do not know why the Cambridge Editors read "runaway's" in the singular. The considerations adduced will, I hope, justify us in reading—

> Spread thy close curtain, love-performing night,
> That *runaways'* eyes may wink.

Act v, scene 1, line 1—

> If I may trust the flattering *truth* of sleep,
> My dreams presage some joyful news at hand.

The quarto reads "flattering eye," which is intelligible enough.

On revision, however, the author may have thought it better to adopt a term more in consonance with flattery in its natural sense. But this can scarcely be "truth," as the terms are destructive of each other. "Flattering sooth," Mr. Grant White's conjecture, does not afford sufficient reason for the change, as "sooth" is nothing but "flattery" already expressed. "*Vouch*," I think, will answer the purpose, and account for the author's alteration.

I would accordingly propose—

> If I may trust the flattering *vouch* of sleep.

TIMON OF ATHENS.

Act i, scene 1, line 33—

> how this grace
> Speaks his own *standing*.

The language of the poet introduced in this scene is turgid, and his treatment of the subject he undertakes absurd. His fancy indeed is vigorous; but, without guidance of taste, he runs riot in the indiscriminate employment of mean and exalted images.

Thus he says, line 23—

> Our poesy is a *gum, which oozes*.

Johnson's happy correction for " gowne, which uses "
And line 48—

> My free drift
> Halts not particularly, but moves itself
> In a wide *sea of wax*,

which Hanmer misunderstands of "waxen tables" to write upon. It is an image evidently borrowed from the practice of modelling in wax, as he says, line 46—

> I have in this rough work *shaped* out a man.

and his "moving in a wide sea of wax," describes the breadth and fertility of his own invention.

This peculiarity of his language may make us hesitate before we correct it elsewhere, but the words, "how this grace speaks its own *standing*," convey no meaning.

"Standing" is probably a mistake for "seeming." So *Puttenham*, page 268, Ed. Arber. "[For] this good *grace* of everything in its kind," the Latin's "*decorum*," our own Saxon English term is "*seemliness*."

Thus *Cymbeline*, Act i, 6, 168—

> He sits 'mongst men like a descended God,
> He hath a kind of honour sets him off,
> More than a mortal *seeming*,

Winter's Tale, iv, 4, 74—"These keep *seeming* and savour, all the winter long."

The poet, when he says—

> "how this grace
> Speaks his own *seeming*,"

declares it requires no speech to point out its excellence.

Act iii, scene 6, line 78—

> The rest of your *fees*, O Gods, the senators of Athens, together with the common *legge* of the people.

For "legge," Rowe's conjecture, "lag," has been commonly accepted. It seems to have authority, as I see Cotgrave so translates the word "dernier," in the phrase "le dernier le loup mange"—"The lag (or laziest) of a flock is preyed on." This, however, only goes to justify it in the sense of "laggard," which is scarcely appropriate to the passage here, which rather requires "the dregs." "The dregs of the people" is a common expression. Cotgrave gives it with the explanation "Racaille canaille."

If Singer's conjecture, "lees," were adopted, it would strongly confirm a similar term, "dregs," in the second place. But I do not see how Timon can say, "The rest of *your* lees, O Gods." This objection does not hold to the same degree against "file." He proceeds by names of multitude, "a score of villains," "a dozen women," and then comprehends the mass.

So *Coriolanus*, i, 6, 42—

>   but for our gentlemen,
> The common *file*.

Measure for Measure, iii, 2, 139—

>   The greater *file* of the subject;

we might then read—

>   The rest of your *file*, O Gods, the senators of Athens, together with the common *dregs* of the people.

Act iv, scene 3, line 12—

> It is the *pastour* lards the brother's sides,
> The want that makes him *leave*.

"Pasture" and "lean" are obvious alterations made by Rowe in the one case, and the second folio in the other.

I do not see why "brothers" should not be allowed to stand, as it is in just keeping with the principal idea, of variety of fortune separating those most closely connected by Nature—"Twinned brothers of one womb." That *feed* makes fat, and want makes lean, without this further contrast, is very commonplace.

But whether we read "rother," or "wether", or "brother," I cannot but think "want" requires correction. In country parishes the "Pasture and arable ground" was protected, as it is now fenced. The unprotected land around is called "Waste." This will redeem the lines from platitude—

> It is the *pasture* lards the brother's side,
> The *waste* that makes him lean.

JULIUS CÆSAR.

Act iv, scene 1, line 34—

"And *in some taste* is Lepidus but so."

The expression "in some sort," meaning "in a high degree," is so common in our author, that, as it suits the sense here, it may plead a title to replace "in some taste," which, if it have any sense, must mean rather "in a low degree." A "taste" is the prelude to a fuller measure, and means "a little." I do not conceive that "taste" can possibly be used for "sense," as if he meant "in a certain sense."

I say "in some sort" commonly signifies a great degree, as I think appears from *Timon of Athens*, ii, 2, 181—

> And *in some sort* these wants of mine are crowned,
> That I account them blessings,

Titus Andronicus, iii, 1, 39—

> "Yet *in some sort* they are better than the tribunes,"

and in other places, though in some again the superlative sense is less evident.

The same observation may be made on Shakspere's use of the word "partly," which though admitting, of course, of less or more, is most commonly used for the greater part, and means "much," "mainly," or "principally."

Thus in *Coriolanus*, i, 1, 35, "to be *partly* proud, which he is *to the altitude* of his virtue."

It is, it is true, contrasted with "chiefly" in *Romeo and Juliet*, v, 3, 28—

> Why I descend into this bed of death
> Is *partly* to behold my lady's face,
> But *chiefly*, &c.

But "I partly think," "I partly know," in *Measure for Measure*, v, 1, 443, *Twelfth Night*, v, 1, 116, signify what we call a moral conviction as distinct from positive evidence.

In this use "partly" only just falls short of "entirely," as it is employed in *Merchant of Venice*, iii, 2, 227, "They are *entirely* welcome." "Entirely" is found, with "love," to express the highest degree possible, *Much Ado*, iii, 1, 36—

> "But are you sure
> That Benedick loves Beatrice so *entirely?*"

So *Lear*, i, 2, 92, "To his father, that so tenderly and *entirely* loves him," *i.e.*, "with all his heart," in which sense it is found in our Communion Service, "We *entirely* desire Thy fatherly goodness."

This sense of "partly" as something short of "entirely" is still in use in the country. Miss Baker, in her "Northamptonshire Words," gives it "Partly: almost, nearly," "*Partly* as usual," *i.e.*, "nearly as usual." "He's *partly* ten years old," almost ten years of age. Often used as a termination to a sentence which conveys a positive assertion. "The boy's as much like his father as if he were the same over again, *partly*." I can myself bear witness to her accuracy as regards "Partly as usual," *i.e.*, "much as usual," the constant answer of an old parishioner of mine to my enquiry after his health.

I do not know whether these peculiarities in the sense of "partly" "in some sort" has been adverted to by critics. I think they may justify the change in the text, though that of this play is so ordinarily correct, to—

"And, *in some sort*, is Lepidus but so."

MACBETH.

Act iii, scene 4, line 103—

> "Or, be alive again,
> And dare me to the desert with thy sword;
> If trembling I inhabit *then*, protest me
> The baby of a girl."

I cannot but think that critics who have attempted corrections of this passage have overlooked the most obvious one of all. "Inhabit" is constantly joined with adverbs of place, "here," "there," "where," and in the text "*then*" is, I conceive, nothing but a mistake for "*there*." And we should read—

> "If trembling I inhabit *there*."

"Desert" which just precedes suggests to the author the word "inhabit"; which is indeed also used without such direct reason for its employment as in *Richard III*, Act i, 4, 29—

> "and in those holes
> *Where* eyes did once *inhabit*."

Instead of saying "dare me to the desert, and if I tremble there," which would have been simple prose, our author gives a fanciful and poetical turn to it, "dare me to the desert, and if I am a trembling inhabitant of it"; which perhaps the strength of passionate appeal renders less natural under the circumstances, but which is too much in his manner to offend us.

The connexion of "desert" with "inhabit" in this place leads me to refer to another where it is found alike, and where I think it has been equally misunderstood.

In *As You Like It*, iii, 2, 115, the folio reads—

> Why should this *desert* be,
> For it is *unpeopled?* No;
> Tongues I'll hang on every tree
> That shall civil sayings show.

Orlando asks, I conceive, "Why should this place, because it is desert in one sense of the word, viz., uninhabited, 'for it is unpeopled,' be desert in the further sense of wild and 'uncivilized'?" "No," he replies, "it shall not, I will hang tongues on trees to teach civility."

This sense is obscured to say the least by altering the punctuation as the Cambridge Editors—

> Why should this a desert be?
> For it is unpeopled? No, &c.

If stress be laid on "*this*," to give it the value of

a whole foot, there will be no need of any other change but the suppression of the comma, and we should read—

> Why should this desert be
> For it is unpeopled? No, &c.

Act iv, scene 3, line 84—

> This Avarice
> Sticks deeper, grows with more pernicious root
> Than summer-*seeming* lust.

"Seeming" in the sense of "seemly" (see note on *Timon of Athens*, i, 1, 33) is entirely out of place, and what other it can bear more appropriate to the context it is hard to guess. "Summer-teeming," Warburton's conjecture, is much nearer the purpose as intimating the effect of the heat of passion. But as lust is the passion itself, perhaps "summer-swelling" may be the word. It has the authority of *Two Gentlemen of Verona*, ii, 4, 158—

> "The summer-*swelling* flower."

Act v, scene 8, line 54—

> MACD. Hail, King! for so thou art; behold, where stands
> The usurper's cursed head; the time is free,
> I see thee compassed with thy kingdom's *pearl*,
> That speak my salutation in their minds.

It is difficult to conceive how a pearl can compass anything. The word refers to the noblemen and soldiers who surrounded Macduff, as is clear from the following line. Malone interprets it "his kingdom's ornament," which might perhaps be tolerable if there were no better solution. But as by their saluting him king, after the "usurper's" death, they acknowledged themselves his *kingdom*, it seems much more natural to read "pale."
So in *Henry V*, Act v, chorus—

> "Behold the English beach
> *Pales* in the flood with *men*."

Again in *Richard II*, Act iii, 4, 40—

> Why should we in the *compass* of a *pale*
> Keep law and order.

I would therefore read—

> "I see thee *compassed* with thy kingdom's *pale*."

◆◆◆◆◆◆◆◆◆◆◆◆

F

HAMLET.

Act i, scene 1, line 84—

>   in which our valiant *Hamlet*,
> For so this side of our known world esteemed him,
> Did slay this Fortinbras.

One can scarcely believe that the author would make Horatio expend a whole line on justifying his epithet "Valiant," as applied to the deceased king. It seems much more likely that he gave him a name of honour, which required such warranty. "As valiant as *Hercules*," occurs in *Much Ado*, iv, 1, 318, and 1 *Henry IV*, Act ii, 4, line 260, and Horatio may be supposed to call him so. This is in some degree supported by Act i, 2, 152—

> My father's brother, but no more like my father
> Than I to *Hercules*.

Act i, scene 4, line 36—

>   "The dram of *eale*
> *Doth* all the noble substance *of* a doubt
> *To* his own scandal."

Mr. Grant White's remark, that possibly the

corruption of the passage lies in the word "doth," induces me to add another to the numerous conjectures which have been made, hitherto without any signal success.

I would, with diffidence, suggest that "doth" ought to be "draweth." "Eale" is most easily, I think, altered to "evil;" though "ill," or "base," which have been also proposed, will serve the purpose equally. The only further correction needed will be to transpose the prepositions "to" and "of."

Hamlet says, the corruption of a part throws suspicion on the whole. This sense will follow on he reading proposed—

> "The dram of *evil*,
> *Draweth* all the noble substance *to* a doubt
> *Of* his own scandal."

Act iii, scene 4, line 161, from the quarto—

> "That monster, custom, who *all sense* doth *eat*,
> Of *habits devil* is angel yet in this;
> That to the use of actions fair and good,
> He likewise gives a frock or livery
> That aptly is put on."

The word "likewise," of the fourth line, indicates that the "giving a frock or livery" has been already implied in the preceding words; and we can easily detect it in the word "habit," of the second. But the words, "all sense doth eat," must be grossly corrupted if they were intended to have any connexion with the idea of clothing.

I think "all" is a mistake for "ill," and "eat" for "coat," which will further entail the change of "sense" to "deeds," and the transposition of "habit" and "devil."

We shall then have the following—

> That monster, custom, who *ill deeds* doth *coat*
> In *devil's habit*, is angel yet in this,
> That to the use of actions fair and good,
> He likewise gives a frock or livery
> That aptly is put on.

Act iv, scene 5, line 131—

LAER.   only I'll be revenged
         Most throughly for my father.
KING.   Who shall stay you?
LAER.   My will, not all the world,
         And for my means, I'll husband them so well,
         They shall go far with little.

Laertes means that as far as his *will*, resolution, and determination of avenging his father's death is concerned, the whole world should not deter him. And as regards his *means*, he lets the King know he is not so unprovided but that he *can* carry his determination into effect.

It is a line of great importance as contrasting the instantaneous resolution to be stopped by nothing in his attempt to avenge his father's death, on the part of Laertes, with Hamlet's apparent vacillation under similar circumstances.

This is unfortunately obscured in the Cambridge Edition, by reading with a colon—

> My will, not all the world :

as if the Editors understood that Laertes meant nothing but his own will should stay him. There should be nothing but a slight pause to distinguish "will" and "means."

If the punctuation be changed at all, it should be only by a semicolon—

> My will, not all the world ;
> And for my means, &c.

Act v, scene 2, line 110 (from the quarto)—

> To divide him inventorially would dizzy the arithmetic of memory, and yet *but yaw* neither, in respect of his quick sail.

Hamlet means, I apprehend, the utmost effort of memory, though it made the mind dizzy, would yet come far behind the enumeration of his excellencies.

"Yare" is used for "agile," or "quick," in several places as *Twelfth Night*, iii, 4, 214, "Be *yare* in thy preparation, for thy assailant is *quick*." It seems to have been especially employed in nautical language. *Tempest*, i, 1, 6; *Antony and Cleopatra*, iii, 7, 38; which recommends its adoption here, where "quick sail" follows immediately. "But" is apparently a mistake for "be not."

I would accordingly propose—

"To divide him inventorially would dizzy the arithmetic of memory, and yet *be not yare* neither, in respect of his quick sail."

Act v, scene 2, line 207—

If it be now, 'tis not to come; if it be not to come, it will be now: if it be not now, yet it will come; the readiness is all, since no man *has* ought of *what* he leaves. What is't to leave betimes?

The substance of Hamlet's reflections seems to be the uncertainty of the time *when* we shall die, whence he infers that all times are pretty much alike if only we are ready; and therefore as well betimes as later.

We may obtain this sense by borrowing "knows" from the quarto, and changing "what" to "when," and read—

> The readiness is all, since no man *knows* aught of *when* he leaves.

KING LEAR.

Act i, scene 1, line 70—

> I profess
> Myself an enemy to all other joys
> Which the most precious *square* of sense professes.

"*Precious square of sense,*" whether it "professes" or "possesses" joys is, I suppose, alike unintelligible. Hanmer's emendation of "spirit of sense," has the authority of *Troilus and Cressida*, i, 1, 55, and iii, 3, 105, in which passages it seems to mean "delicate sensibility," "refined and subtle sense," by a legitimate oxymoron: "spirit" and "sense" being in reality opposed to each other, as "flesh" and "spirit" in Scripture.

Regan, however, must apparently rather mean that she professes herself an enemy to all joys which sense can promise, or hold out the expectation of. This will be obtained by reading "*shape of sense,*" as we find it in *Troilus and Cressida*, i, 3, 386—

> But, hit or miss,
> Our projects life this *shape of sense* assumes,
> Ajax, employed, plucks down Achilles' plumes,

i.e., the success of our project takes this shape, or

gives this *reasonable* expectation, "sense," being used for reason.

Regan will use "sense" in its proper acceptation as the source of "joys," and declare she professes herself an enemy to all joys which sense professes to bestow in the most *precious shape* they take of imaginary delight.

According to this, we must retain "professes," and read—

> I profess
> Myself an enemy to all other joys
> Which the most precious *shape* of sense professes.

Act iii, scene 7, line 58—

> The sea with such a storm, as his bare head
> In hell-black night endured, would have *buoyed* up
> And quenched the *stelled* fires :
> Yet, poor old heart, he holp the heavens to *rain*.

For "*buoyed*," which can mean nothing, and for which Warburton proposed the trivial and obvious emendation "boiled," the quartos read "laid," or "layed," which though equally destitute of sense, point to the probable word, viz., "*leaped*."

For "*stelled*" fires, the quarto reads "*steeled*," which is equally unintelligible, but points to the word "*sheeted*." "Sheets of fire" have already been spoken of, Act iii, 2, 46.

For "*rain*" the quarto reads, I believe, correctly, "rage."

Thus corrected, the passage will run—

> The sea with such a storm as his bare head
> In hell-black night endured, would have *leaped up*
> And quenched the *sheeted* fires,
> Yet, poor old man, he holp the heavens to *rage*.

Act iv, scene 6, line 271—

> O undistinguished *space* of woman's will!
> A plot upon her virtuous husband's life;
> And the exchange my brother.

"Space of woman's will" is unintelligible. The epithet "undistinguished," *i.e.*, "undistinguishing," gives reason to believe that the word "space" is nothing but a mistake for "choice," which is further supported by the word "exchange."

"Will" is "passion" or "desire," as we find it in *Othello*, iii, 3, 236—

> Foh! one may smell in such a *will*, most rank,
> Foul disproportion,

and in *Cymbeline*, i, 6, 45—

> The cloyed *will*,
> That satiate and unsatisfied *desire*.

Hamlet, in Act iii, 4, 73, where he reproaches his

mother with conduct almost exactly analogous to Goneril's in this play, says to her—

> Madness would not err,
> Nor sense to ecstasy was ne'er so thralled
> But it reserved some quantity of *choice*
> To serve in such a *difference*.

"Choice" has besides peculiar propriety in the text, as "choice" is an exercise of "will."
I would on these grounds suggest—

> "O undistinguished *choice* of woman's will."

OTHELLO.

Act ii, scene 1, line 26—

"A Veronesa."

Steevens' supposition that the name of the ship is intended, derives some support from a similar incidental name of a palace, "The Sagittary," i, 1, 158; i, 3, 115. If so perhaps it would be "The Veronica," after the saint who wiped our Lord's face on his way to Calvary.

Act iii, scene 3, line 169—

O beware, my lord, of jealousy;
It is the green-eyed monster, which doth *mock*
The meat it feeds on.

The only interpretation of this as it stands must be, I suppose, that jealousy mocks, *i.e.*, as we might say now in low style, "makes a fool of" the person affected by it, or as we might again say, "who is eaten up with it"; which might possibly be allowed as intelligible if jealousy were alone in question. But the idea of a "monster" "mocking" the food he eats is incongruous. Theobald's conjecture "makes" is open to objection on the same score, that it applies well enough to jealousy which derives its nourishment from itself, and often creates its own suspicion; but it will not pair with "monster" any more than "mocks." Besides, Iago's purpose is not to suggest to his master there was no ground for jealousy, that it was his own creation; but to humiliate him by recommending him to be secure, and not trouble himself with it.

In *As You Like It*, Act ii, 5, 36, we have—

> "*Seeking* the food he eats,"

which implies trouble and labour in search of it, a meaning which will suit "jealousy" and "monster" alike.

We might read perhaps—

> It is the green-eyed monster, which doth *seek*
> The meat it feeds on.

Act iv, scene 2, line 55—

> A fixed figure for the time of scorn
> To point his slow unmoving finger at.

See note on *Henry V*, Act i, scene 2, line 93.

Act iv, scene 3, line 25—

> My mother had a maid called Barbara;
> She was in love, and he she loved proved *mad*,
> And did forsake her.

If Desdemona could possibly say "proved mad," I can only conceive she was thinking of her own husband, who was "mad" with jealousy, and that she attributed the same aberration to Barbara's lover. But the song only says "False love." To make "mad" mean "false" by the intermediate sense of "wild," as has been proposed, is an extremely forced interpretation. It would be more probable that the word itself was in fault. We might substitute "naught," which is found in an analogous sense in *Romeo and Juliet*, iii, 2, 85—

> There is no trust,
> No faith, no honesty in men: all perjured,
> All forsworn, all *naught*, all dissemblers.

Act v, scene 2, line 85—

> OTH. Being done, there is *no pause*.

This must mean, I suppose, "When once the deed is done, there is no longer waiting for it"—a sense, which if it bear any relation to the occasion in Othello's mind, is certainly no answer to Desdemona's entreaty. She beseeches him to pause "but half an hour." It would be natural for him to reply in the bitterness of his soul, that after the deed was done there would be a longer pause than "half an hour"—an eternal one; and this will be intimated if we read—

Being done,
There's *pause eno'*.

ANTONY AND CLEOPATRA.

Act i, scene 2, line 155—

> When it pleaseth their deities to take the wife of a man from him, it shows to man the tailors of the earth, comforting therein that when old robes are worn out there are *members* to make new.

This passage has been left unintelligible, as far as I can judge; for "tailor," as Pope reads for "tailors," and "numbers" for "members," as Hanmer, do not make the meaning any clearer.

Enobarbus, I fancy, is making allusion to the Destinies or Fates with their shears and thread, and grotesquely calls them the "Tailors of the earth," whose business it is to *mend* old clothes, or make new. This, I think, is further supported by words following, "Then had you a *cut* indeed."

I would accordingly propose "*menders*" for "*members*."

Act ii, scene 5, line 99—

MESS. Take no offence, that I would not offend you;
To punish me for what you make me do,
Seems much unequal : *he's married to Octavia.*
CLEO. Oh, that his fault should make a knave of thee,
That art not what thou'rt sure of!

The numerous emendations of the text, which fail to satisfy, make it allowable to suggest that the error lies not in the word, but in the division of the speeches.

The messenger is unwilling to incur Cleopatra's fury by repeating the unwelcome assurance of Antony's marriage. He does nothing but ask her pardon, and deprecate her anger. The words, therefore, "He's married to Octavia!" can scarcely belong to him. They are, I apprehend, the last of Cleopatra's indignant enquiries, upon which the messenger, having exhausted his excuses, stands mute, confused, and uncertain what to say. Thereupon Cleopatra taunts him as a "knave," for suppressing the message he was entrusted with, as if by his amazement he pretended he was "not sure" of a matter of which he was perfectly sure. She alludes to the common evasive reply, "I'm not sure."

According to this we should divide as follows:—

MESS. Take no offence that I would not offend you,
To punish me for what you make me do,
Seems much unequal.
CLEO.   He's married to Octavia?
[The messenger pauses and makes no answer.]
O that his fault should make a knave of thee,
That art not what thou'rt sure of!

G

Act ii, scene 6, line 68—

    POM.   And I have heard Apollodorus carried——
    ENO.   No more of that: he did so.
    POM.   What, I pray you?
    ENO.   A certain queen to Cæsar in a mattress.

It is hard to understand what Enobarbus can mean by trying to suppress a topic by the words, " No more of that," and then continuing to narrate it.

It seems as if in this place again there is a faulty distribution of parts. In the next scene, line 6, the servant describes Lepidus, "He cries out, '*no more*,' reconciles them to his entreaty, and himself to the drink," which justifies us in supposing that it is he who endeavours to stifle the scandal, and we should divide as follows:—

    POM.   And I have heard Apollodorus carried——
    LEPIDUS.   No more of that.
    ENO.   He did so [aside to Pompey.]
    POM.   What, I pray you?
    ENO.   A certain queen to Cæsar in a mattress.

Act iii, scene 9, line 8—

                At such a point
    When half to half the world opposed, *he being*
    The *meered* question?

Dr. Abbott defends the possibility of "meered" being used for "mere," as if it meant "he being the *entire* question," section 394. One would think Shakspere might in that case have easily said, "He being the only question," and avoided so uncouth a term. Besides the construction then gives two nominatives absolute, "world to world opposed," and "he being," as forming a sentence, which in its degree may be deemed further evidence of corruption in the whole passage.

"Question" may be used for "contest" or "dispute," as in *Hamlet*, v, 2, 362, "So jump upon this bloody question," and then "meered" may be a mistake for "mortal," as we find "mortal arbitrement" in *Twelfth Night*, iii, 4, 249. "Being" may represent "begins," and "he" be needlessly introduced.

The lines would then run—

> At such a point
> When, half to half the world opposed, *begins*
> The *mortal* question, 'twas shame no less, &c.

Act v, scene 2, line 7—

> Which sleeps, and never palates more the *dung*,
> The beggar's nurse and Cæsar's.

But for the Cambridge Editors' adoption of

Warburton's conjecture of "dug" for "dung" I should have deemed it indefensible.

The Duke in *Measure for Measure*, Act iii, 1, 13; in his depreciatory remarks on human life, analogous to Cleopatra's here, observes—

> Thou art not *noble*,
> For all the accommodations that thou bear'st
> Are *nursed* by baseness;

and we have already in Act i, scene 1, line 35—

> Our *dungy* earth alike
> *Feeds* beasts and men.

Cleopatra says, "Death sleeps," and is no longer exposed to the vulgar exigencies of mortality, from which a Cæsar is not free any more than the beggar.

Act v, scene 2, line 120—

> I cannot *project* mine own cause so well
> To make it clear.

If "project" be retained it can only mean, I suppose, "put forward"; but such a sense is not supported by any similar use of the word by our author, who uniformly uses it as a noun for "purpose" or "design."

"Proctor," Warburton's ingenious, but rather tasteless conjecture, is equally inconsistent with Shakspere's use, who would have said "attorney."

I would suggest the word "perfect," in the sense of "free from blame or guilt," by the analogy of *Measure for Measure*, v, 1, 80—

> When you have
> A business for yourself, pray heaven you then
> Be *perfect*,

and *Othello*, i, 2, 30—

> My parts, my titles, and my *perfect* soul,
> Shall manifest me rightly.

Cleopatra says, "She cannot free herself from the imputation of guilt, so as to *clear* her honour."

> I cannot *perfect* mine own cause
> To make it clear.

Act v, scene 2, line 213—

> Saucy lictors
> Will *catch at* us like strumpets.

"Catch at," though allowed by all editors, does not commend itself by any convenient sense. Perhaps it is an error for "chastise," which was accented on the first syllable. So we read 1 *Henry VI*, i, 5, 12—

"But I will *chastise* this high-minded strumpet."

See *Lear*, iv, 6, 158.

Act v, scene 2, line 228—

> *Sirra*, Iras, go,
> Now, noble Charmian, we'll dispatch indeed.

"Sirra," or "sirrah," cannot, I apprehend, be spoken to Iras, on account of her sex, and her mistress's affection, which alike forbid its application, and there is no one else present but she and Charmian. Very probably it is an error for "swift," which is countenanced by "dispatch" in the next line.

> *Swift*, Iras, go,
> Now, noble Charmian, we'll dispatch indeed.

CYMBELINE.

Act i, scene 5, line 16—

> Ay, and the approbation of those that weep this lamentable divorce, under her colours, *are* wonderfully *to* extend him; be it but to fortify her judgment, which else an easy battery might lay flat, for taking a beggar *without less quality.*

This confused sentence might be made grammatical if we read—

> "Ay, and the approbation of those that weep this lamentable divorce under her colours: *who* wonderfully *do* extend him, be it but to fortify her judgment, which else an easy battery might lay flat, for taking a beggar *without less quality*";

in which reading I adopt Eccles' change of "do" for "to," but change "are" to "who."

"Without less quality" evidently means without "more" quality, but there is no need to alter the form of expression, as there are many instances where "less" and "more" are interchanged without strict logical propriety—a practice it may be useful to illustrate.

It appears in *Lear*, ii, scene 4, line 196—

> his own disorders
> Deserved much *less* advancement,

i.e., the gallows, which was *more* than the stocks.

It is true it may be interpreted as if the stocks being less dishonourable than the gallows, hanging were a less advancement in point of honour. But this seems too subtle an interpretation. "Advancement" is used in a sense analogous to the verb "advance," viz., "elevate."

Again, *Troilus and Cressida*, Act i, scene 3, line 70—

> And be't of *less* expect
> That matter needless, of importless burden,
> Divide thy lips, than we are confident,
> When rank Thersites opes his mastic jaws,
> We shall hear music, wit, and oracle.

Agamemnon means "We may *more* reasonably expect Ulysses to babble, than Thersites to speak wisdom."

Again, *Coriolanus*, Act i, scene 4, line 13—

> Tullus Aufidius, is he within your walls?
> 1 SEN. No, nor a man that fears you *less* than he:
> That's lesser than a little.

Here logical propriety requires "more than he":

but the sense of "fearing little," and "less than little," prevails over strict logic.

As we find "less" used for "more," so "more" is often found where we should expect "less."

E.g., Timon of Athens, Act iii, scene 5, line 82—

> If by his crimes he owes the law his life,
> Why, let the wars receive't in valiant gore ;
> For law is strict, and war is nothing *more;*

i.e., nothing *less*.

Again, *All's Well That Ends Well*, Act i, scene 3, line 154—

> Or were you both our mother
> I'd care no *more* for't than I do for heaven,
> So I were not his sister.

Helena says if the Countess were mother of both Bertram and herself it would no *less* satisfy her longing than heaven itself would.

I have adopted Capell's reading, "I'd care no more for't," instead of " I care no more for," which change this use of "*more*" strongly supports, and I read " mother " for mother*s*, as " both our mother " for " mother of us both " seems better grammar. "Your three motives to the battle," in Act v, 5, 388, *i.e.*, "The motives of you three," is an instance of similar construction, in the present play.

Again, *As You Like It,* Act ii, scene 3, line 10—

> Know you not, master, to some kind of men
> Their graces serve them but as enemies?
> No *more* do yours :

i.e., no less.

These instances of "no more" where we should say "no less," are, however, where they express similarity, or equality, just as correct as our modern use. Where Sir Philip Sidney says in his Apology for Poetry (p. 46, Ed. Arber), "It is sung but by some blind crouder, with no rougher voice than rude style," though we should say, "with no *less* rough a voice than rude style"; there is no difference in the meaning, the "roughness" and "rudeness" being "equal."

In the passage of the present play, which has given occasion to these remarks, the word "extend," *i.e.*, "enlarge" or "magnify," which precedes, may account for the logical impropriety; the author probably intending a contrast to that term in the word "less."

Act i, scene 6, line 23—

> "Reflect upon him accordingly as you value *your* trust."

Though "your trust" is not unintelligible in the

sense of "the trust reposed in you by us," it will be much clearer if we read "our trust," *i.e.*, "the trust I repose in you."

Act iii, scene 2, line 70—

> I have heard of riding wagers,
> Where horses have been nimbler than the sands
> That *run* in the clock's behalf.

A match against Time in which the horse won seems to be intended. In this case, as the horse *ran* in the man's behalf, the sands are considered to do so on behalf of Time, or the clock which rang the hour.

It is possible "run" may be used as a perfect for "ran," but as I know no examples of it, I would propose to change it to "ran."

> I have heard of riding wagers,
> Where horses have been nimbler than the sands
> Which *ran* i'the clock's behalf.

www.ingramcontent.com/pod-product-compliance
Lightning Source LLC
Chambersburg PA
CBHW022147160426
43197CB00009B/1468